Michael Kimball

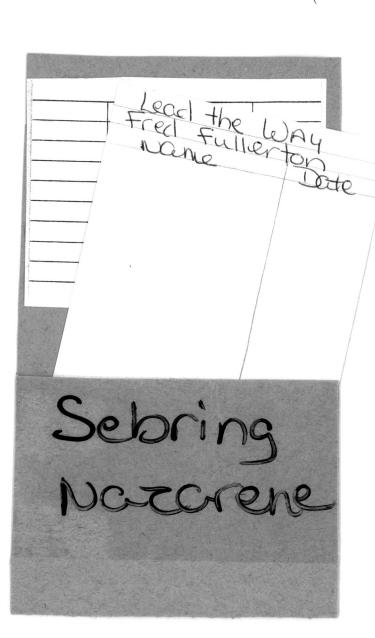

Lead the WAY
Fred Fullerton
Name   Date

Sebring
Nazarene

Lead the Way

28 Devotionals for Christian Teens— Emerging Leaders

Fred C. Fullerton

Beacon Hill Press of Kansas City
Kansas City, Missouri

10   9   8   7   6   5   4   3   2   1

To
my daughter Carla,
an emerging young leader

Preface

Lead the Way. It is a call to young people like you to provide leadership for your generation and the church in this critical decade of the 1990s. God has always called upon the young to provide leadership at important times in history. The list of names from the pages of Scripture sound like a "Young Leader Hall of Fame" roster: David, Jeremiah, Esther, Daniel, and Timothy, to name a few. In their time, and their place, they responded to the call of God and provided vision and energy and commitment. That's leadership.

The same is true today. God is raising up a whole new generation of young leaders to take on the "giants" of this age with faith and boldness. He is looking for students like you.

Me, a leader? Not! That was the first response of many whom God used in the past. But those who, after prayer, responded to His call made an incredible difference in their world.

God qualifies those He calls. He prepares a person for leadership. He develops leaders from the inside out, working on their character and commitment.

The purpose of this devotional book is to assist you in your personal spiritual development as a young leader, in your time, the 1990s, and in your place (community, school, and church). For the next 28 days I challenge you to commit the time to read the Word, to reflect on the devotional, and to pray. As you do, God will *lead the way* for you, and He will begin to show you how He wants you to *lead the way* for others to Jesus Christ in your world.

TIPS FOR EMERGING LEADERS TO FOLLOW WITH THIS BOOK

Here are a few tips that will assist you in getting the most out this devotional book:

Commit a time—Select the best time of the day for you when there would be approximately 15-20 minutes of uninterrupted time to work through the devotional exercise.

Commit a place—Pick a place in your home that will become your special place to meet with God in the next 28 days. Discipline yourself to use the same place each day.

Begin with prayer—Start your time with God with a word of praise and a request for understanding of what He wants to say to you through the Word and the devotional.

Use your Bible—Each day a passage of Scripture is to be read from your own Bible before you read the devotional thought for the day. Some are brief; some include entire chapters. Read just one devotional a day, and place a checkmark on the page after you are done to note your progress.

Memorize Scripture—I challenge you to memorize the scripture highlighted at the end of the devotional. It is the verse(s) for the day or verse(s) from a larger passage of Scripture that has been selected. Your spiritual life will be strengthened through the memorizing of God's Word.

Reflect—Think back on what you have read and begun memorizing. Space has been provided at the bottom of each page for you to either write out the scripture you are memorizing or a brief thought that comes to mind. Think about what God is teaching you throughout your day. Meditate upon Him anytime, anyplace.

Respond—Take specific action in response to what God is teaching you. Put the Word into practice.

Develop a prayer partnership—While time spent alone with God is vital, the support and accountability found with a prayer partner is a great encouragement to follow through with commitments you made, or to share insights gained. Challenge a friend to join you in these 28 days—and beyond! You may want to start a small prayer group in your home or at school.

LEAD THE WAY.

READ: 2 Tim. 3:16-17

As a kid in Sunday School I remember singing a chorus that went something like this: "The B-I-B-L-E, / Yes, that's the Book for me; I stand alone on the Word of God, / The B-I-B-L-E! Bible!" The children's teachers were trying to impress on our young minds just how important the Bible is to believers in Jesus Christ. That was good teaching then, and it is still true today. You've just read two verses of Scripture that reinforce what I was taught in that Sunday School class. God's Word has a purpose, a mission. The major mission is to help us come to know Jesus as Savior and Lord.

All parts of Scripture are useful in one way or another. Some parts focus on helping us understand what God is like. Other scriptures help us know how to live God's way. Through the Word we get a grip on what we are to be like, and we are prepared for the things God has for us to do.

Unfortunately, I have found that many people, both young and old, who call themselves Christian spend little time in the Book. Recently, I returned from Russia, where I helped distribute Bibles in Moscow. For almost 70 years, the people of the Soviet Union were forbidden to own Bibles. Christians had hidden theirs, if they had one, or had torn it up into smaller portions to share with other believers. To Russian Christians, the Word of God is a very precious thing.

If you haven't been using your Bible lately, find it and dust it off, or buy yourself a new one. There are many great Bibles for Christian teens available. Carry it to church. Use it in the services. Make notes in the margins of things you want to remember or questions you have. Read it at home. Help start a Bible study group at your school. Why? God inspired it and had it written for you and for those who don't yet know Him. And as an emerging leader, soak His Word up and allow it to continue the transformation process begun when you asked Jesus into your heart. The B-I-B-L-E. Make it the Book for you.

MEMORIZE 2 Tim. 3:16-17—Jot it down or write a thought you've had.

PRAY: *Jesus, during these four weeks and beyond, help me soak up Your Word so that I may be trained in righteousness and equipped for every good work.*

READ: John 14:23-24

I love basketball. I played it in elementary school (my rural school had all eight grades in it), high school, and two years in college. It was great fun. Wearing the uniform, hearing the crowd and pep band, getting pumped for the competition, the smell of popcorn, and much more all came together at tip-off time.

In the days leading up to each game, there was practice. In practice we would work on physical conditioning and skill drills. Fundamentals. The basics included dribbling the ball, passing, free throws, rebounding, and many others. These skills had to be kept sharp if we were to perform well in the game. Practice wasn't as much fun as the games. But when game time came, it would become crystal clear which team on the court had put their heart into practice that week.

In the passage you read, Jesus is dealing with one of the basic elements of Christian discipleship—obedience to His teachings. This obedience flows from a heart that loves Him. Basic. Fundamental. Because I love Him, I obey His teachings. I find those teachings in His Word. I also find those teachings being lived out day by day by believers who form my community of faith, the faith team known as the church.

With the practicing of the basics, like obedience, comes the promise that God the Father, God the Son, and God the Holy Spirit will make my heart Their home. That is presence. That is fellowship. That is sweet!

Maybe it's time to get back to some basics in your spiritual journey—Scripture reading, prayer, fellowship, service. God will show you if you let Him. The choice is yours. Those who truly love Him obey His teachings, and those who don't, don't. That's basic.

MEMORIZE John 14:23—Jot it down or write a thought you've had.

PRAY: *Jesus, help me stick with the basics. Give me the desire and grace to obey Your teachings. Forever make my heart Your home.*

A WISE TIME-OUT

READ: Luke 5:15-16

"Time-out! Time-out!" I screamed as loud as I could at the referee after our opponents scored. Just seconds remaining. Down by one point. The final play that would determine the outcome of the championship game would be called in our huddle. My teammates and I listened closely as we wiped the perspiration from our faces with towels and grabbed a quick sip of water from the squeeze bottles. The tension was high. "Pressure-ville."

Time-outs. Time-outs are invaluable to both players and coaches. They are used by coaches to draw a team together, to focus on the next play or series of plays to be used in the effort to defeat the opponent. Strategy is adjusted. Players rest. And they make mental adjustments in their personal performance.

Scripture has told us that as often as possible Jesus made it a priority to withdraw for a time to pray. A wise time-out. Why? As Jesus' ministry continued to grow, the demands upon His time grew rapidly as well. He knew that if He was to stay focused on His ultimate mission—going to the Cross to die for the sins of the world—that He would have to stay in tune with the Father. From those times in prayer Jesus gained the strength to keep on keeping on. He was renewed within His spirit and refreshed in mind and body.

As His disciples, we must do the same. We have busy schedules. Many demands are placed on us by school, friends, family, youth group, jobs, extracurricular activities, etc. And we, too, are on a mission for God in this world—to make a difference, to share the Good News, to be a person of spiritual influence among our peers.

Regardless of the many commitments, for an emerging Christian leader, one commitment must be constant. That is the commitment to take a wise time-out to spend time with Jesus in the Word, and in prayer and listening. We went on to win the game I mentioned in those last few seconds. A wise time-out made it possible.

MEMORIZE Luke 5:16—Jot it down or write a thought you've had.

PRAY: *Jesus, help me to find a quiet place for my daily time-out with You. Help me not only to read and pray but to listen too.*

READ: Luke 16:13

God won't compete for your attention or loyalty. He alone is to be No. 1 in our lives. Think about it. Check out the Old Testament Book of Exodus, chapter 20, and verse 3:

"You shall have no other gods before me."

It is the first commandment of the Ten Commandments given by God to Moses on top of Mount Sinai after leading the emerging nation of Israel out of bondage and slavery in Egypt. God established the ground rules for how He would relate to them and they to Him. He did that because of His love for them, and ultimately for everyone who would come to know Him through Christ, His Son.

We are commanded to love God with an undivided heart. And what was true in the Old Testament for the nation of Israel was restated once again in the words of Jesus that you read in Luke 16:13.

Jesus understood that there are many things that attempt to compete for our attention, our energies, and our loyalties in this life. Legitimate things. Things that are necessary, like money. It is when money becomes our first love, when money is thought of more often than anything else, when we sacrifice time with Him (time in worship and fellowship) in order to earn money, that Jesus calls us to remember we can truly serve only one master.

Many high school students work part-time. If you are one of them, check your motivation for working. Are you assisting your family by working? Is it solely for additional spending money? Is the commitment to work taking you away from church services and youth activities? Are you tithing on your income? To be a genuine disciple of Jesus, you must consider these questions and pray for God's guidance. You, too, can serve only one master. Follow Him with an undivided heart.

MEMORIZE Luke 16:13—Jot it down or write a thought you've had.

PRAY: *Lord, help me not to buy the lie that I can serve two masters. Make me aware of anything that is competing with You for first place in my life; then help me to take action to change.*

READ: John 13:34-35

A friend of mine served the church for a time as a missionary in Germany. Randy and his wife, Lori, started a coffeehouse ministry to young people. In time, the Lord helped them touch a number of lives with the gospel. The group grew. More lives were transformed through the love of God.

One night following a service, a man who was walking by the coffeehouse stuck his head in the door, attracted by the noise and laughter of the young people. Seeing the man, Randy went to him and introduced himself. He explained what the group was about. The man nodded his head and then made an interesting observation. He said to Randy, "Where's there's love, it's loud!"

What do you think he meant by that comment? One thought I've had is that it is pretty obvious when people really care about others. There is a freedom to laugh, to have fun, to enjoy the fellowship of true Christian friends. Acceptance. Respect. Love. It's a good place to be.

Think about your youth group for a moment. What is the prevailing attitude? Positive? Open? Fun? How would a passer by describe your gatherings? How are new students received by you and your friends? Are they welcomed, or perceived as a threat to somebody's "turf"?

The type of love that Jesus is referring to in John 13 is a love characterized by acceptance, support, forgiveness, listening, sharing, and time invested in building caring relationships. In a world full of broken homes, broken dreams, and broken spirits, your youth group can become a safe place, a good place, a redemptive place for those who do not know Jesus Christ. Take action. Lead the way. Talk to your peers and youth leaders about the quality of love and fellowship in the group. From time to time we all need an attitude check. The commandment is clear—love one another, as Jesus has loved you.

MEMORIZE John 13:34—Jot it down or write a thought you've had.

PRAY: *Jesus, help me do what I can to make my youth group like that coffeehouse in Germany. Check my attitude toward others. Help me love others as You have loved me.*

QUESTIONS WELCOMED, RESPONSE REQUIRED

READ: Judg. 6:11-24

Have you ever questioned God? You are not alone. Have you ever wondered if it was really God speaking to you specifically? In the Old Testament passage of Scripture you have just read, a young man named Gideon is working and minding his own business when suddenly an angel of the Lord appears. Not your typical day. The angel's first words were a bit different as well: "The Lord is with you, mighty warrior."

"Are you talking to me?" is in essence Gideon's reply. If you are, and, "if the Lord is with us, why has all this happened to us? Where are all his wonders that our fathers told us about when they said, 'Did not the Lord bring us up out of Egypt?' But now the Lord has abandoned us and put us into the hand of Midian" (Judg. 6:13).

During this period in Israel's history, the nation faced a series of foreign armies who attempted to conquer it. Israel also fell away from its commitments to God, and the judges were specific people God raised up to lead the nation in battle and in spiritual renewal. Gideon struggles when he see all the problems around him. He questions where God is in all this mess. God's response to this questioning is patience, and a call to *lead the way* for his people. "The Lord turned to him and said, 'Go in the strength you have and save Israel out of Midian's hand. Am I not sending you?'" (v. 14). Gideon responds, Who, me? Look, I'm nobody. But the Lord persists and promises to be with him, giving him one final sign. Gideon is convinced the Lord really is talking, really is calling, really is empowering to carry out the task. Later we read that with the odds overwhelmingly against him, Gideon and his men triumphed over their enemies.

Questions welcomed, response required. God wants to hear your questions, your doubts, your fears. But He also expects a response, an action on our part when He makes it clear that He has a job for us to do. *Lead the way*, in the strength He will give you.

MEMORIZE Judg. 6:14—Jot it down or write a thought you've had.

PRAY: *Lord, give me the boldness to ask You the questions that are on my heart, and the courage to carry out Your calling on my life in the strength You give.*

FARMER GOD

READ: John 15:1-8

I lived in the state of Idaho for four years. It is a great place. While Idaho is known for its famous potatoes, the state also produces large quantities of fruit, especially apples. Delicious.

Portland, Oreg., is an eight-hour drive west on Interstate 84 from where I lived in Nampa, Idaho. Along the way, one passes several apple orchards. One fall morning while on my way to Portland, I came upon a sight I had never seen before. An apple orchard alongside the highway near the Oregon state line looked like it had been the recent site of an amateur chainsaw-users convention. The once-beautiful trees looked like skeletons. Creepy. Skinny. Huge piles of branches lay at the base of each tree. It didn't look good. Trust me.

I learned later that what looked like disaster was part of the process of raising good apples. The farmer was doing what was best for his trees. Pruning. He was cutting back the branches so that the tree would not expend its energy solely on growing branches, but on the buds that would emerge in the spring. This pruning is good for the tree, and in turn, good for the farmer because his apple crop will be more "fruitful," so to speak.

You have already made the connection with today's scripture reading. God is the Farmer. Jesus is the True Vine, the Source of our spiritual life. We are the branches. If we are going to produce good fruit, we need to be attached and pruned. We need to be in right relationship with Christ. Separated, we can't produce anything. The pruning is initiated by the Farmer for our good. He loves us. He cares for us. He desires to see us reach our full potential in and through Him.

Stay attached to the True Vine. Respond to the pruning of the Farmer God with obedience. Say yes to areas of your life He wants you to change. Say yes in anticipation of greater growth and maturity. And say yes with joy, knowing that what He is doing is best for you.

MEMORIZE John 15:5—Jot it down or write a thought you've had.

PRAY: *Father, pruning sounds radical. I want to say yes, and I want to grow. Help the yes to grow stronger. Give me grace to embrace the changes coming for my own good and the good of others. I love You.*

FOR SUCH A TIME AS THIS   MONDAY • 8

READ: The Book of Esther

If you were assigned the responsibility for promoting the Book of Esther to be read by your friends, what title would you give it? "Small-Town Girl Rules"; "My Uncle with the Weird Name"; "Capital City Star-Search"; "Don't Mess with Es(ther)"; what's your entry? (I'm sure it is better than the above!)

Whatever the "tag" might be, this story demonstrates the faithfulness of God and His confidence in young people to *lead the way* when the times are tough. Esther had no idea what God had in store for her when she emerged as the king's choice to replace the former Queen Vashti.

Crunch time emerges in chapter 4. The plot to destroy all the Jews throughout the kingdom had been found out by Esther's uncle Mordecai (love that name). Esther receives word from him that she needs to go to King Xerxes "to beg for mercy and plead with him for her people" (Esther 4:8). No can do, replies Esther. Without an invitation from the king, even the queen doesn't show up for an audience. But Uncle Mordecai won't take no for an answer (read vv. 12-14).

Esther can be part of God's rescue plan, or she can check out. It's her choice. Read her reply:

Then Esther sent this reply to Mordecai: "Go, gather together all the Jews who are in Susa, and fast for me. Do not eat or drink for three days, night or day. I and my maids will fast as you do. When this is done, I will go to the king, even though it is against the law. And if I perish, I perish" *(4:15-16).*

Read the rest of the story if you haven't. A teenage girl was entrusted with incredible responsibility to make a difference. She struggled, prayed and fasted, and stepped out in faith, believing God was leading her. Her obedience led to boldness that resulted in deliverance. To this day Israel celebrates Purim, a day of deliverance because of Esther and the faithfulness of God. The church today needs thousands of young women and men like Esther. Will you be one?

MEMORIZE Esther 4:14b—Jot it down or write a thought you've had.

PRAY: *Strengthen my faith, Lord. Help me make a difference too.*

16

TUESDAY# TO TELL THE TRUTH TUESDAY • 9

READ: Eph. 4:25

My favorite television program after church on Sunday night was "To Tell the Truth." It was a game show where the object was for a "panel of experts" to determine which person among three was really the person introduced, the one telling the truth about who they were and what they did. The panel had to wear blindfolds and were allowed to ask a series of questions during each round of play.

Unfortunately, telling the truth has waned in popularity and practice. A recently published book titled *The Day America Told the Truth* claims that 91% of Americans admit they lie routinely; some 86% lie to parents regularly, 75% to friends, 73% to siblings, and 69% to spouses. It also says that some 81% of Americans lie about their feelings!

What has been your experience? Do you feel that people regularly lie to you? Have you felt pressure to lie to someone recently? Has it become routine for you? Is it more or less acceptable in your youth group?

The apostle Paul instructs the believers in the church at Ephesus to speak the truth. No more lies. Why? Because that is what Jesus would do. Because in the Church, Christ's Body, we are all connected to one another. So when you lie to others, you basically end up lying to yourself. Not smart. Not spiritual. Not a good witness to those outside the church.

Mart De Haan of the Radio Bible Class from Grand Rapids, Mich., writes:

> If I lie, I have believed that it is up to me to save my own skin. I have assumed that it is safer to distrust God than to run the risk of being found out by others. I have forgotten that because of the mercy of Christ, telling the truth is **always** safer than telling a lie.*

Make a commitment to "talk straight up" to everyone you encounter. *Lead the way* in integrity. Be known as a person who can be trusted. Honor God by observing the ninth commandment, "You shall not give false testimony against your neighbor" (Exod. 20:16). Tell the truth.

MEMORIZE Eph. 4:25—Jot it down or write a thought you've had.

PRAY: *Lord, when tempted to lie or shade the truth for my own advantage, check me and help me be a person who always tells the truth.*

---

*Mart De Haan, "Thinking About Telling the Truth," *Times of Discovery*, August 1991. Copyright 1991 by Radio Bible Class. Used by permission.

READ: Rom. 12:14-15

Playing varsity basketball in high school was a great thrill for me—a dream come true. As a kid I remember going with my dad to the high school gym. It seemed huge. A large sign hung on the far wall behind the basket: HOME OF THE OTTAWA PIRATES. I decided then that I wanted to be a Pirate and make baskets and hear the crowd cheer. For Christmas that year I got a basketball and a bright orange goal with a net. My dad held the basket (two feet off the floor) as I tried to throw the new ball into the goal. That's a good memory for me.

Playing varsity basketball was a great thrill but also a challenge to my faith. I was one of the few players who attended church regularly and the only one who didn't go drinking after the games. I had promised my father before he died from cancer when I was a freshman that I would never drink alcohol or smoke. He asked me to do that because he loved me and knew the dangers associated with those habits. He didn't want me to get caught up with a group of friends that would pull me away from church and God. Some of you reading this know exactly what I'm talking about. My dad's concern and call to abstinence is still valid in the 1990s.

Driving home alone after games when the rest of the squad was together doing the drinking thing wasn't easy. It hurt, even though I knew I was doing the right thing. The good news was that my friends at church and my pastor were there for me and helped me stick to my commitments.

In the years that have passed, I have met young people around the world who face incredible persecution for their commitment to Christ. I have been blessed by their joy in the face of hurt and rejection. I have been challenged by their practice of praying for those who put them down.

This is what the apostle Paul was getting at in verse 14 of Romans 12. Bless your enemies, pray for them. Endure the insults. They really don't know how lost they are, and God wants them to come to faith. (Footnote: In writing this devotional, the Holy Spirit reminded me that on those nights when I drove home alone, there was another Passenger in the car.)

MEMORIZE Rom. 12:14—Jot it down or write a thought you've had.

PRAY: *Help me face persecution and be to others what You are to me.*

A UTILITY POLE AND
A VOICE YOU CAN TRUST

READ: John 10:1-18

I had heard about it for weeks. The ropes course. "Challenging," "fun," "a real test for anyone" were some of the comments given me by those who had endured. I could wait. Heights didn't frighten me. *Falling* from those heights did. I'm not into pain and full-body casts.

I was the chaplain for the college, and I thought I could support the students in prayer from the lodge. They don't need me on the ropes course site, right? Wrong. Nobody gets to ditch the course. Everyone was to participate in this "team-building" experience for the student leaders and student development staff.

Nearly 50 of us, students and staff alike, walked out into the woods from the lodge to the ropes course location. We received instructions and were divided into groups of 8. The final challenge of the day was the 30-foot utility pole climb. I'd love to meet the guy who designed this one. In short, climb the pole, balance yourself on top standing up straight, leap to a ring of iron lashed between two trees, then let go of the ring with both hands as you are lowered down by a cable attached to your safety harness. No problem! It became a problem as I reached the top of the pole to stand up while balancing my body—when I froze. I could not move. I was overcome by fear.

The students and staff below were all yelling encouragement to me. I wanted to meet the challenge, but fear was winning out. I was about to come down when I heard one voice above all the others. It was a voice I recognized and trusted, Roger Schmidt, women's basketball coach and close friend. My mind blocked out everything but Roger while he gave me specific instructions. He kept telling me I could make it. One last time I stood up on top of the pole, balanced myself, and jumped to grab the ring six feet away. I had conquered the challenge and more importantly my fear.

The voice of the Good Shepherd is one you can trust, in the midst of the many voices heard daily. He laid down His life for you. He will lead, encourage, and make a way for you. His is the Voice you can trust.

MEMORIZE John 10:11—Jot it down or write a thought you've had.

Voice you can Trust

PRAY: *Help me know Your voice from all the rest. Guide me.*

READ: 1 Cor. 10:13

During a trip to Los Angeles in November of 1993, I saw from my airplane window some of the wildfires that were sweeping through the canyons and hillsides along the southern California coast. The fires were rapidly driven along by high winds known as the Santa Anas. Hundreds upon hundreds of homes were destroyed and over $200 million in damages were caused by the fires. The extent of the devastation in some areas was hard to comprehend.

Thanks to the dedication and bravery of firefighters, many lives were saved and homes spared from the stubborn fires. Nightly news carried story after story of the firefighters facing incredible odds and risking their lives to provide a way out for persons and livestock trapped by the blazes.

A way out. It is the first thing one looks for when physical danger emerges. I remember my high school driver's education teacher telling the class over and over, "Always leave yourself a way out when you're driving in traffic." To this day I drive in either the far outside or far inside lane in case I need to take to the ditch or shoulder area to avoid an accident if at all possible. I try to give myself room to escape a crash.

A way out is what the Christian must look for when spiritual danger arises. Temptation is common. Every believer is tempted at some point and from time to time. Satan is real and is the enemy of our soul. In a matter of moments, you can land in a situation where it seems like sin has you surrounded like a wildfire and there's no way out. Don't give in. Stop. Pray. Think. Exit. As the Scripture passage says, God will provide a way out.

The growing Christian will begin to recognize more quickly and with greater spiritual discernment (radar) the situations that should be avoided to lessen the threat of spiritual danger. Be alert. God will provide the exit option at just the right time.

MEMORIZE 1 Cor. 10:13—Jot it down or write a thought you've had.

PRAY: *Open my eyes to those situations that set me up for spiritual defeat. Sensitize my mind and heart. Keep me alert to the way out that only You can provide when temptation comes.*

CHANGED FROM THE
INSIDE OUT

READ: Rom. 12:1-2

The enemy of our soul, Satan, is the author of lies and deceit. He uses our contemporary culture as one of his tools in the ongoing effort to pull us away from God. As one of my youth-pastor friends puts it, Satan attempts to get people addicted to something. He sells the lie that you are what you look like, or what you accomplish, or what you want, or what you own—that's living in a culture of deceit.

Read carefully the Romans 12 passage below:

So here's what I want you to do, God helping you: Take your everyday, ordinary life—your sleeping, eating, going-to-work, and walking-around life—and place it before God as an offering. Embracing what God does for you is the best thing you can do for him. Don't become so well-adjusted to your culture that you fit into it without even thinking. Instead, fix your attention on God. You'll be changed from the inside out. Readily recognize what he wants from you, and quickly respond to it. Unlike the culture around you, always dragging you down to its level of immaturity, God brings the best out of you, develops well-formed maturity in you *(TM)*.

"Changed from the inside out" is the work of the Holy Spirit in our lives. He makes us aware of those areas of our lives that are pleasing to God and those areas that need to be worked on with His help. He gives us God's desires. He empowers us to live clean lives in a mud-stained world. He transforms us by the renewing of our minds and spirits.

Think about what is important to you. Is Satan attempting to get you hooked on one of the addictions mentioned above? It all seems pretty harmless at first, but in time, the desire for God begins to lessen, and the desire for the things that please you increases. Take action today. Invite the Holy Spirit to change you from the inside out. He is ready to free you, to cleanse you right now.

MEMORIZE Rom. 12:1-2—Jot it down or write a thought you've had.

PRAY: *Search my heart just now. Identify anything that is beginning to compete with You for first place. Change me from the inside out, by Your grace.*

DARE TO DISCIPLINE—
YOURSELF

READ: 1 Cor. 9:24-27

I love the Olympic Games. The finest athletes in the world perform under incredible pressure and the constant eye of the television camera. Years of training have been invested for events that last only minutes.

The apostle Paul was familiar with such athletic events in the Greek cities. He was also familiar with the discipline required to compete successfully. Athletes usually trained under strict supervision for 10 months prior to annual games. They were required to observe a rigid diet.

In the Scripture reading for the day, Paul draws on his knowledge of the games and training routines to make several points. First, a believer in Christ must master his or her body and not allow the body to be master. The Corinthian believers, prior to coming to salvation in Christ, had been participants in practices where the body was master. Drunkenness and sexual immorality had been part of their pagan worship rituals. As Christians, they were to live differently. Their bodies now were temples of the Holy Spirit. They were to discipline themselves.

Next, Paul wanted to communicate how important it is to finish the race begun with Christ because the crown, or "gold medal," received at the end is eternal. It will never fade or tarnish like the awards given in his day and ours.

Spiritual disciplines, such as prayer, fasting, tithing, and being a faithful participant in worship are needed if we are to survive and grow as disciples. Physical disciplines such as regular exercise, good eating habits, and adequate sleep are necessary for our personal health. Make a checklist of the disciplines, both spiritual and physical, that you are keeping now. Make a separate list of those you would like to begin in the next 30 days. Ask a parent, friend, or youth leader to hold you accountable. Dare to discipline yourself.

MEMORIZE 1 Cor. 9:24—Jot it down or write a thought you've had.

PRAY: *Lord, help me to be more self-disciplined in all areas of my life.*

READ: Rom. 12:12

On a scale of 1-10, with 10 being incredibly patient, where would you rank yourself? A 3, or a 9 possibly? Me? I'm basically an impatient person at heart. I want to get a job done and get on to the next project. My dad would say to me that I was great at taking things (my toys) apart, but I didn't have the patience to put them back together.

Webster's dictionary defines patience as "the will or ability to wait or endure without complaint; steadiness, endurance, or perseverance in performing a task." It is a quality that we all need to be part of our life.

I did a word search in the Bible on the word "patient" and found some interesting verses. Here are a few to think about:

Prov. 14:29—A *patient* man has great understanding, but a quick-tempered man displays folly.

Prov. 16:32—Better a *patient* man than a warrior, a man who controls his temper than one who takes a city.

1 Cor. 13:4—Love is *patient*, love is kind.

2 Pet. 3:9—The Lord is not slow in keeping his promise, as some understand slowness. He is *patient* with you, not wanting anyone to perish, but everyone to come to repentance.

There are countless opportunities that come our way that challenge us to be patient. Finishing a tough class at school, learning a new skill, developing a meaningful relationship, paying back a loan, or finding God's will for your life are just a few of those opportunities.

In the believer's journey, patience is developed through a growing dependence upon God. More and more I must turn to Him to help me in every area of my life. Patience promotes the development of perseverance, of hanging tough when it seems everything bad is happening to or around you. And most of all, we must be as patient with ourselves as He asks us to be with others. Give yourself some grace, give others grace, and just try to be patient. It comes through practice.

MEMORIZE Rom. 12:12—Jot it down or write down a thought you've had.

PRAY: *Help me to be patient with others, and myself, as You continue to be patient with me.*

READ: Phil. 2:3-11

Check it out! Stand by the entrance to your school, and you will find someone walking in with an attitude. I'm talking about the "strut your stuff, I am cool" attitude. Do you know anyone like that? It's a power thing, a selfish thing, that is usually driven by peer pressure or insecurity. What else should we expect from those who do not know Jesus Christ as Savior? Our society, with its upside-down set of values, promotes such attitudes.

Those who follow Jesus Christ by faith are to be different. We are to get our attitude from His example. Here's another version of the beginning verses of the passage you just read:

Don't push your way to the front; don't sweet-talk your way to the top. Put yourself aside, and help others get ahead. Don't be obsessed with getting your own advantage. Forget yourselves long enough to lend a helping hand. Think of yourselves the way Christ Jesus thought of himself. He had equal status with God but didn't think so much of himself that he had to cling to the advantages of that status no matter what. Not at all. When the time came, he set aside the privileges of deity and took on the status of a slave, became *human!* Having become human, he stayed human. It was an incredibly humbling process. He didn't claim special privileges. Instead, he lived a selfless, obedient life and then died a selfless, obedient death—and the worst kind of death at that: a crucifixion *(TM)*.

I am encouraged by your generation! Your involvement in service projects, your concern for the environment, your compassion for the homeless, and your investment in caring for the elderly give me hope for the future of the church. These activities reflect an attitude that reflects Christ.

Keep putting others first. It is not popular and not convenient. Remember, Jesus didn't take His directions from the culture but from the Father. Pride divides. Humility unites. Get an attitude—from Christ!

MEMORIZE Phil. 2:3—Jot it down or write a thought you've had.

PRAY: *Jesus, it's attitude-check time. Help mine to reflect Yours.*

READ: 2 Cor. 1:3-11

One of my high school friends shared his basic outlook on life with me on the way home from basketball practice. It was a little rhyme that went like this:

When the tide of life goes against you,
And the waves upset your boat,
Don't worry about the way things might have been,
Just lie on your back and float!

OK, it's a little lame to say the least, but at the time it was funny.

The apostle Paul would not have been blessed by this perspective. He had been shipwrecked three times and on one occasion spent a night and a day in the open sea. In addition, he had his share of hard times as he carried out the mission God had given him to preach to the Gentiles. Beatings, imprisonment, persecution, and the constant need to assist the churches that had been started under his ministry were part of the pressures he faced.

In spite of all he faced, Paul talks about the "God of all comfort." The idea he conveys is that God stands beside a person who is undergoing severe problems. God's presence and comfort is not just for a short time but is constant, no matter what the problem. And the comfort doesn't just equal the stress caused by the problem; it overwhelms it. It is like comparing the water pressure of your garden hose to Niagara Falls—God's comfort is that much greater.

The good news is that the pressures we face can be used by God for a purpose—to teach us to depend on Him more and more. It's a choice. We can depend on Him or on ourselves or others. The comfort comes when we choose Him.

And there's more! What happens when a friend goes through "high tide times"? The comfort we have received can be shared as encouragement. Never underestimate the power of your presence in the name of Christ in the life of a friend. Your presence and prayers are mighty resources God uses to help one face the tide in stride. (Check out Rom. 8:38 too!)

MEMORIZE 2 Cor. 1:5—Jot it down or write a thought you've had in the space below.

PRAY: *In the "high tide times" in my life or in the life of a friend, help me to seek Your comfort, to really depend on You.*

READ: Nehemiah 1—2; 4—6

Thanks for reading through five of the first six chapters of this great Old Testament book. (Some wild names, eh?) Nehemiah was a young man. Due to the destruction of Jerusalem by invading armies and the exile of its citizens, Nehemiah finds himself in the capital city of a foreign king, a servant in the palace.

Nehemiah caught a vision from God following several days of fasting and prayer (1:4). Radical! The vision leads to specific action when in chapter 2, Nehemiah asks King Artaxerxes for permission to visit Jerusalem, to rebuild the city walls, to replace the gates, AND to get the wood for the project donated from the king's own forest! Huge requests—but the king agreed to them all because God had granted Nehemiah favor with the king.

The vision and God's answers to prayer kept Nehemiah focused on the goal of rebuilding the walls and gates. Think about your youth group and your church for a moment. Anything needing to be "rebuilt"? Relationships? A sense of unity? New classrooms? The youth group itself? Pray and seek God's direction. Become a part of the solution and be a voice for vision and change.

We can learn several things about what a leader will face and must do from Nehemiah's experience (check out the verses listed):
- Leaders will face opposition. (4:7-8; 6:1-13)
- Leaders must identify the problem and respond with a plan. (4:9)
- Leaders must strengthen the followers' faith. (4:14)
- Leaders must stick with the task God has given them to do. (4:15)

I challenge you and your youth group to study the Book of Nehemiah over a three- to four-week period. Pray that God will give you a vision for what He wants to see accomplished through the group. You could reenergize your local church with your enthusiasm and dreams! *Wanted: Young Leaders with Vision!* Will you be the one?

MEMORIZE Neh. 1:11—Jot it down or write a thought you've had below.

PRAY: *Help me become the leader my youth group and church need at this time.*

HONOR GOD WITH YOUR "BOD"   FRIDAY • 19

READ: 1 Cor. 6:18-20

Sexuality. God created it. That makes it good. God gave it to men and women to enjoy in a special relationship—that of marriage. He did so because there is much more to sex than mere skin on skin. The false message we get from our pagan society would make us believe that the physical act is enough. It is not. That thinking results in an immoral lifestyle that lacks intimacy and commitment, and leads to deep loneliness and deadly diseases.

One's sexuality is an expression of who a person is. It is part of one's identity. We are sexual beings, but our sexuality is a gift and is to be guarded closely with the help of the Holy Spirit. It reflects the Creator God who made and gave us our "bods."

This is why the apostle Paul speaks so strongly about sexual sins. Our bodies are not our own. They are the place where the Holy Spirit lives. Every believer is a temple in which God resides. Our lives, lived out through our bodies, are to give glory to God. This must rule out all behavior that is not appropriate to the temple of God.

I know you've heard this a million times. But truth is worth repeating. There's too much at stake. I know of too many young people whose lives have been devastated by becoming sexually active before marriage. You most likely know someone too. When people become involved in sexual immorality, they not only sin against their own bodies but also sin against Christ himself, and the Church, the Body of Christ on earth.

The good news is that forgiveness is available to those who have become involved sexually, and God's grace is available to help those who want to save themselves sexually for their marriage partner. Being a virgin is a tremendous treasure to bring into marriage. God's way is the best way.

Respect yourself, respect your date, and honor your future lifelong mate by honoring God with your body.

MEMORIZE 1 Cor. 6:19-20—Jot it down or write a thought you've had below.

PRAY: *Thank You for the wonderful gift of my body, my sexuality. Help me glorify You by guarding the gift.*

THOUGHT TRACKS SATURDAY • 20

READ: Phil. 4:8-9

Research time. Record the focus or topic of your thoughts for 10 minutes, or longer if you wish. Write them down. Divide your list into two categories—positive and negative. Circle the positive ones and put a star by the negative. Add them up. Which one had the most?

I hope the positive group had the most. Unfortunately, many young people, if asked to do this same activity, would have the larger number in the negative category. Why? First, they are bombarded every day by negative information about the world. Street violence, world hunger, natural disasters, and disease are seen or heard about, to name a few. Second, they are often hit with negative comments from their parents or friends. "You're lazy," "You're not smart enough," "Can't you do anything right?" "You are a real geek!" or much worse, is some of the input received. Negative input leads to negative thinking. Fortunately, the reverse is true as well.

The Philippian passage challenges Christians to focus their thoughts on the good. We are to fill our minds on things that are true, noble, reputable, real, encouraging, excellent, or worthy of praise. These things exist in large numbers too.

Stop! Reality check! Who are you kidding? Get a grip! Look around you— Open your eyes! Didn't you read what you wrote in the last paragraph? Yes, I know what I wrote. The apostle Paul is not saying to close our eyes to the incredible pain and suffering in the world. Believers are to be salt and light. We are to make a difference. Serve the needy. Shelter the homeless. Feed the hungry. What Paul is calling us to is a transformation of our thinking patterns. The salvation of Christ changes everything. We can become positive people in the midst of negative events and challenges. It is the power of God at work within our life and mind that can redirect our thought tracks.

MEMORIZE Phil. 4:8—Jot it down or write a thought you've had below.

PRAY: *Jesus, redirect my thought tracks. Transform negative thinking into positive. Help me focus more on the good things about You, others, and myself.*

THE CONTINUING MISSION   SUNDAY • 21

READ: 2 Cor. 5:16-20

"Star Trek." I grew up watching the original program that had Captain Kirk and Mr. Spock on the bridge of the Starship *Enterprise.* "Star Trek: The Next Generation" has been fun for our daughter Carla and me to watch in recent years. I love the phrase Captain Picard uses at the beginning of the show in reference to the Starship *Enterprise*—"its continuing mission . . . ," and you know the rest. The time, the crew, and the ship are all different from the original show, but the mission of the *Enterprise* is still the same.

Continuing mission. On a much more serious level than a TV series, you are part of God's continuing mission of reconciliation. That means He is taking the initiative to reestablish a relationship that has been broken, in this case, by sin. He wants everyone to be saved.

You are an official ambassador for Jesus Christ. You are His representative to your peers at school, and to your family members who may not know Christ in a personal way. An ambassador's responsibility is to communicate effectively and precisely the message given by one's superior. You've been entrusted with the message of hope and eternal life in Christ!

Here are the facts: God makes His appeal to others through you and me. If someone gets saved, it starts in somebody else. When I stop to really think about this, I am humbled. God chooses you and me to represent Him! Unbelievable! What a privilege!

Let's bring it closer to where we live—who among your family or friends is not a Christian? Think of them right now. Pray for them. Pray that God will give you and other Christian ambassadors opportunities to build bridges of love to them. Think of opportunities to invite them to a Christian concert or a special church service. Get them acquainted with your pastor, Sunday School teacher, or youth pastor. And watch God work through *your* life! The mission God began thousands of years ago continues, and you're a key part.

MEMORIZE 2 Cor. 5:20—Jot it down or write a thought you've had below.

PRAY: *Lord, help me represent You faithfully to my family and friends.*

29

READ: Heb. 12:1-3

If you have never been to a stadium for a major university or professional sporting event, I hope you will have the opportunity soon. I live in Kansas City. The Royals are an American League baseball team and the Chiefs are a National Football League team that call Kansas City home. The teams each have their own beautiful stadium side by side at the sports complex. It is much different being there in person than watching the event on the tube at home. There is an energy, an enthusiasm that is present that is fun to be a part of and certainly is encouraging for the home team.

This passage in Hebrews starts off with a statement that more or less says there is a "hometown crowd" of followers of Christ cheering us on from heaven. We can't see them or hear them, but they are there cheering for us. They are the faithful believers who have gone on to their heavenly reward, and they're quite interested in how we are doing.

If we have that type of great crowd encouraging us, then the writer to the Hebrews says we need to respond by doing three things:

1. **Get on with it!** The clock is ticking! Throw off the warm-up suit and run! Discipline yourself and discard anything that could drag you down during the race.
2. **Don't quit!** Never, never, never quit! Run the course with your mind fixed on the goal.
3. **Keep focused on Jesus.** He ran this race, actually started it and finished it. Review the race films (study the Word) to see how He did it. He never lost sight of where He was headed because He knew it would be worth everything He would have to endure.

And if you get discouraged, remember that your fans are watching—and that they made it. But most of all, remember Jesus. Review the tape, step-by-step. It will inspire you again!

MEMORIZE Heb. 12:3—Jot it down or write a thought you've had below.

PRAY: *Help me gain encouragement to stay in the race from the "hometown crowd" and from You, who finished so that I could run it.*

READ: Titus 2:11-14

There you are, standing in a long line at the theme park you've dreamed of going to ever since you were a kid. The most incredible ride in the park is next. You're nervous. You've heard the ride makes people freak. Palms are sweaty, but you are trying to look cool. A group of students exits the ride and walks past your row laughing and, from all appearances, pumped about the ride they just had. An adult three people behind you calls out to the group walking by and asks the question you were wanting to ask, "Was it worth the wait?" "Yo! It was awesome," is the reply. Your heart begins beating a bit faster, and you are pumped, but cool.

Worth the wait. It is always a good feeling to know that your efforts and patience are going to pay off. To see Jesus face-to-face one day is definitely going to be worth the wait. To see loved ones, grandparents, uncles, aunts, and for some, parents or siblings will be one of the many incredible blessings of heaven. Right now that is hard to imagine because nothing we have experienced is like that. That's why young people don't think about heaven much. No problem. One day you will.

In the meantime, while we are waiting for His return without really thinking about it that much, God's grace is helping us live our lives in ways that honor and please Him. That grace helps us say no to "ungodliness and worldly passions, and to live self-controlled, upright and godly lives in this present age, while we wait . . ."

We don't say no out of fear or guilt. That approach does not lead to a healthy spiritual life. We grow and mature by getting rid of everything that is not pleasing to Christ and by adding those attitudes and practices that Jesus had. As we do this more and more, we are freed to be who God intended us to be when we were created.

MEMORIZE Titus 2:11-12—Jot it down or write a thought you've had below.

PRAY: *Thank You for loving me and for giving me the desire to live my life like You want it lived.*

READ: 1 Sam. 16:7

What do you think of your appearance? Tough question. Few people feel good about the way they look. I didn't my freshman and sophomore years in high school. Zits took over my face, and I was so skinny that I looked like a scarecrow. In an attempt to gain weight before sophomore football season started, I started drinking strawberry milkshakes with three to four eggs in them for the protein. At the first practice I'd gained three pounds. But after the first full week I'd lost nine. So much for milkshakes.

Our culture is addicted to outward appearances. Some people try to put weight on, and others try to sweat it off, both in an effort to improve on "the look." Some students I know have taken it so seriously that they have become ill through avoiding food to lose weight and have become anorexic, requiring hospital care and counseling.

We get caught in the comparison trap, and Satan goes to work on our self-esteem. "If I only had her wardrobe," or, "I'd give anything to be built like him," we think. Advertising on TV and in magazines reinforces the feeling that we have to have "the look" to measure up.

Christians are called to focus on the inner life rather than the outward appearance. Don't get me wrong; we are to take care of ourselves. But we're not to become obsessed with ourselves. The Scripture reading reminds us that God doesn't consider us by our looks, but by the condition of our heart. (For some harsh words from Jesus directed to religious people of His day who had the right look but wrong heart, check out Matt. 23:27-28.)

Real friends will accept you for who you are as a person without "the look," whatever it may be that semester. Work on being genuine, real, yourself. God will help you. It's OK to care about your appearance and to feel good about yourself, as long as you don't become a slave to the effort. Keep it all in perspective and strive for balance. And avoid egg-filled milkshakes!

MEMORIZE 1 Sam. 16:7—Jot it down or write a thought you've had below.

PRAY: *Help me see myself as You see me. Balance my perspective.*

SMALL THINGS, BIG IMPACT

READ: 1 Sam. 17:1-50

Ever heard of the lightweight binocular swimming goggle? Olympians wear them so that they can train anywhere from 15,000 to 20,000 meters a day. Before the invention of this goggle, swimmers could only train 2,000 to 3,000 meters a day before their eyes would become irritated from the chlorine in the water. Largely due to the development of the goggles, world records have been steadily smashed over the past 20 years. Small things can have a big impact.

You have read the story of David and Goliath. David was not a trained soldier. He was a young shepherd boy who was on "sheep duty" while his brothers were in the army. During his time in the hillsides, he had mastered the ability to use his sling and stones to keep predators—including a lion and a bear—away from the flock. His practice there prepared him for the confrontation in the Valley of Elah. Still, he was just a young man.

David, in addition to his sling, had great confidence in God. He believed that just as God had delivered him from large animals in the hills, He would deliver him from this "animal" of a man, Goliath. The God we serve desires to prove himself faithful in the face of tremendous odds. He loves to build a history, a yearbook, of faithfulness in our lives. Our availability and His ability to make a great combination.

There were many bigger, stronger, faster, and better-trained men in the Israelite army that fateful day, but none volunteered to face Goliath. David approached him, not with the weapons of the day, but with a small sling, five smooth stones, and a strong faith in God based upon his personal experience. You know the end of the story. One small, strategically aimed stone, catapulted by one small, well-used sling, had a large impact.

David had attended to the things he could, and left the rest to God. You, too, by paying attention to the little things that can have a big impact in your life, can be called and used of God to stand against the "giants" in the land. Are you available?

MEMORIZE 1 Sam. 17:50—Jot it down or write a thought you've had below.

PRAY: *Strengthen my faith and help me pay attention to the little things that can have a big impact in my life.*

READ: Daniel 6

Perhaps one of the greatest challenges you will face as an emerging leader is the development of a godly character. It takes commitment, discipline, humility, and integrity.

In the story of Daniel we see a young man who lived a life of integrity. In Webster's dictionary under "integrity" there are five synonyms listed: "soundness," "incorruptibility," "completeness," "honesty," and "unity." In short, someone you can trust.

Daniel is a teenager, away from his home and the influence of his parents and friends. He proved himself to be a person who would work hard, learn quickly, and follow through with commitments. He impressed the king, which caused jealousy among his coworkers. His enemies tried to find something to bring legal charges against Daniel to get him out of their way. A great sentence in the last part of verse 4 reads, "They could find no corruption in him, because he was trustworthy and neither corrupt nor negligent." That is a testimony we should all work toward.

Daniel becomes the focus of a plot based on his religious convictions. Even while away from home, he stuck with the conviction to pray to God three times a day, even after it had been declared illegal to do so. He is caught praying and thrown into a lions' den. Big cats, big appetites. But notice the king's words in verse 16 as Daniel is being thrown to the lions, "May your God, **whom you serve continually,** rescue you!" (emphasis added). Daniel's life of commitment had made an impact.

Daniel stood firm with his commitments and saw God provide a solution to the hungry cat thing. He was rescued by an angel of God. Then the king threw his enemies in; but they were not rescued.

We learn to stand up for our convictions from stories like Daniel's. God allows us to face tough tests in order to help shape our character, and to be prepared for larger challenges later in life. Stick to your convictions. Live with integrity.

MEMORIZE Dan. 6:16—Jot it down or write a thought you've had below.

PRAY: *Help me be a person who lives by convictions, no matter the cost, like Daniel.*

VERSES FOR LIFE

SATURDAY • 27

READ: Prov. 3:5-6

Do you have favorite Bible verses? If not, try to find at least one in the next month and memorize it. Throughout this devotional book, you have been challenged to memorize Scripture. Why? Because there is probably no other spiritual discipline more useful or rewarding. Your prayer life will be strengthened, and your attitudes will begin to change. Your mind will be more alert, able to retain more and observe more. Your confidence will grow, and your ability to witness effectively will improve. You have just read my two favorite verses. They are my favorite because the Lord gave them to me as a freshman in college and has brought them to my mind more than any other verses thus far in my life.

Prov. 3:5 instructs us to "Trust in the Lord with all your heart"—not in part, not with reservation, but with everything you've got, trust in the Lord. He is to be the Focus of our trust. Not money, not friends, not anything else. And the God who created the universe can be trusted!

"And lean not on your own understanding." Do not totally trust your intellect, your best guess. Seek the wisdom of Christ every day. I pray for His wisdom daily. I need it. He gives it through prayer, or through a comment from a Christian friend, or even a resource I am working with in my assignment.

"In all your ways acknowledge him, and he will make your paths straight." Through your choices of friends, activities, career, dates, etc., choose carefully. Choose after prayer. Praise Him for His answers. He will point the way. He will help you become a person who knows who you are, who likes who you are, and simply lives life with a peace and joy that shines through.

He will open doors that will take you on an incredible journey, more exciting and challenging than you ever thought possible. He's done that for me. He will do that for you. Trust in the Lord.

MEMORIZE Prov. 3:5-6—Jot them down or write a thought you've had below.

PRAY: *Assist my search for verses for life this month. Make them each very special to me.*

READ: 1 Tim. 4:12

Lead the way. May these words be a wake-up call, a call to spiritual leadership for you. The decade of the 1990s carries the potential for a great spiritual awakening led by young people like yourself. It has happened before in history. Your own ability to lead is greater than you think. It needs more time, training, and practice to develop to its potential, but it won't unless you get involved. As a friend of mine recently said in talking about 1 Tim. 4:12, *Don't wait.* Don't wait to take your discipleship seriously. Don't put your spiritual life on hold until adulthood. The Body of Christ has no junior members. This team has no second string. *You* are in the starting lineup.

Read the words to a song titled "Lead the Way," by Brian White and Don Koch. Ask God to show you how you can *lead the way where you live, attend school, and worship. You can do it with His help!*

Standing on the edge of eternity, watching as the world we know searches for the truth,
Following the wisdom of uncertainty, waiting for an answer to the questions of their youth,
Hanging on the verge of certain tragedy, walking toward an endless night, just too blind to see,
Playing with their own eternal destiny,
Running from the only One who can give them what they need.

And though the way seems right, it brings destruction in the end.
Who will pierce the darkness and take His light to them?

Chorus:
We must lead the way, bringing hope to the hurting;
We must lead the way, sharing His love with the lost.
For the road that we are trav'ling will bring them to the Cross,
But it's up to you and me to lead the way.*

MEMORIZE 1 Tim. 4:12—Jot it down or write a thought you've had below.

PRAY: *Lord, this leadership thing is a bit scary. Calm my fears. Lead the way for me. I'll follow closely so that I can lead.*
